The Original Ghost Walk of Whitby.

The Tour in a Book.

By James J. Browne.

Florun House Press.

Dedicated to Samantha,
Trevor and Sandra.
If they hadn't been complete lunatics
this would never have been possible!

"One can never tire of Ghosts and Angels."
Anon.

FOREWORD.
Of Days Gone By.

The Whitby I remember is a very different place to the one I know today. It was a quiet place with a short season for visitors. Locals still lived in the old town and fishing remained a vital part of the town's economy. It was a place that saw little summer and was covered in the thick smoke of coal fires for nine months of the year.

Outsiders have now bought up all the spare properties in the town centre and pushed the price of dwellings beyond the reach of its indigenous inhabitants. This has changed the character of the town considerably as the enterprises of outsiders have replaced those of the locals. The old Whitby is rapidly becoming a ghost in its own right.

WHITBY

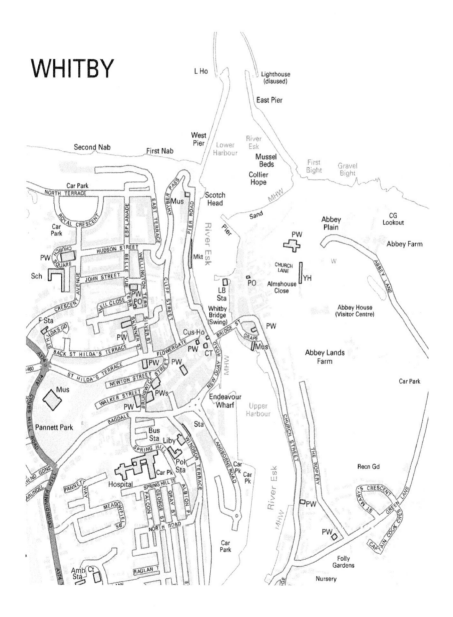

The Original Ghost Walk of Whitby.

Those of who knew the old Whitby remember a slightly battered and windswept place where the pubs closed early and there certainly were no branches of Weatherspoons! Woolworth's still existed and the likes of Sainsbury's and Homebase were a completely foreign concept. The Whitby I remember was a place of strange customs, dark alleyways, long shadows and residents that never travelled out of sight of the abbey.

I was fortunate enough to learn the ghost stories included in this book at firsthand from the locals and used them when I worked as a tour guide. If this book succeeds in embodying something of the spirit of the old town in its content and presentation I will feel my efforts have been fruitful.

I also sincerely hope that if you have not already visited this historical seaside resort you will make the worthwhile effort to visit it at a later date. A map has been included in this book to help you find the locations mentioned in these ghost stories. Logic dictated that I wrote this book as though you were accompanying myself on a "Ghost Walk".

Finally, please don't for one moment think that the Ghost Walk is new fangled invention. The rather surly fisherman, Mr Swales, in Bram Stoker's Dracula spoke of foolish visitors paying to hear nonsense about ghosts and the supernatural – The Original Ghost Walk has a good provenance.

The Original Ghost Walk of Whitby.

Whitby Harbour.

Of Ghosties and Ghoulies.

Mendacem memorem esse oportet.

James J. Browne.

The Pannett Park by moonlight.

CHAPTER ONE.
Bagdale Olde Hall and Dr Ripley's Ghost.

Bagdale Olde Hall.

Good evening, and a warm welcome to the Original Ghost Walk of Whitby. My name is James Browne and I have been a working palmist and clairvoyant for over thirty-five years - so it could be said that my interest in ghosts and the supernatural is rather a professional one. At this point, I would like to sincerely assure you that all the ghost stories you will hear tonight are, to the best of my knowledge, true ghost stories.

We are stood outside Bagdale Old Hall, it is Whitby's oldest intact building and was built in 1516. On an overcast winter evening it develops a cold and oppressive presence and many people find its outward appearance foreboding. Bagdale Old Hall is haunted by the ever present ghost of Captain Brown Bushell who was a successful pirate during the time of the civil wars (1642-1651). Unfortunately, said captain had an ingrained habit of frequently swapping sides between the royalists and the parliamentarians. It was therefore inevitable that he earned for himself the rather dubious honour of being sentenced to death, by beheading, at Scarborough Castle. Brown Bushell's ghostly footsteps can still be heard, with regularity, within the hall's stairways and at nighttime his gruesome headless form can be clearly seen silhouetted against the halls leaded windows.

Naturally enough, Brown Bushell was not the only person with the distinction of being held at Scarborough castle which happens to be a mere twenty-eight miles south of Whitby.

A homosexual favourite of King Edward the Second, the sixth Plantagenet King of England

The Original Ghost Walk of Whitby.

(1284-1327), was imprisoned there before being taken to London for execution. (Incidentally, Edward the Second was the son of Edward "Longshanks" brought to public attention through the film "Braveheart".) This favourite of the King, a commoner known as Piers Gaveston, exerted great influence over his majesty - so much so that the nobleman of the royal court became resentful. Inevitably, a rebellion was encouraged and conducted by the Earl of Lancaster who, legend has it, kidnapped Gaveston and took him to Scarborough Castle where he was sentenced to be beheaded without barely any trial or jury. If you think what befell Gaveston was bad, what happened to Edward the Second was considerably worse; let it suffice to say that it involved a red-hot poker and that the screams were heard two and a half miles from Gloucester Castle. On first hearing of this tale, I felt a Sunday roast would never smell the same again!

To this very day, Gaveston's headless spectre haunts the base of Scarborough Castle walls. Any traveller foolish enough to use the cliff path near the castle on a stormy night is likely to be startled by Gaveston's headless ghost. This apparition will then push them, with astonishing force, over the edge of the craggy cliffs to a most certain death in the crashing waves below.

Just across the road from Bagdale Olde Hall, at the bottom of Brunswick Street (where it meets the end of Baxtergate), is the old MP's surgery. This is quite a fine late Georgian building. However, if you look at it carefully you can see it is only half a building, on the outer edge of it can be seen stone window frames chopped in half and refilled with bricks.

In 1870, there lived within this building a Doctor Ripley. He was, in essence, a very shy and retiring sort of man, he was also a very scientifically minded man and would not admit to a soul that ghosts could possibly exist.

However, Doctor Ripley had a rather serious problem on his hands because within his house there lived a rather obvious ghost. This phantom would appear at his window each evening, overlooking Brunswick Street, and would then amuse itself by leaning out and grimacing at passers-by. Once the ghost had attracted sufficient attention, it would then promptly disappear leaving behind a crowd of astonished onlookers.

Dr Ripley's House.

The Original Ghost Walk of Whitby.

The ghost's appearances and disappearances were so frequent that crowds used to gather outside Doctor Ripley's house each evening to watch it. So great was the apparition's popularity there was even a report about it in the local newspaper, the Whitby Gazette. To use an Irish expression Doctor Ripley was "caught between a rock and a hard place"; he certainly didn't like the crowds gathering outside his house each evening disturbing his peace. However, being a scientifically minded man he couldn't possibly call in a priest, or an exorcist, to get rid of the ghost because that would have been as good as admitting to its existence.

Doctor Ripley's solution to this problem was quite interesting, and rather destructive - he decided to have the half of the house in which the ghost lived demolished! Consequently, you can now see for yourselves, that at the end of Baxtergate, there stands a testimony in bricks and mortar to the existence of spectres.

Relief at Bagdale Olde Hall.

CHAPTER TWO.
The Bargheust Hound.

Harbour view from the west side.

The coastal regions of North Yorkshire are haunted by a terrible Hound of Hell locally known as the Yorkshire Bargheust, or the Bargheust Hound. Such a hound stands between six and nine foot tall at the shoulder, has a coarse black pelt, glaring red saucer like eyes and, of course, lots and lots of teeth within its horrible foaming mouth. This sounds rather like a description of a rabid dog to me! There are versions of this terrifying hound in many parts of the United Kingdom; each of these canines have their own strange names such as Shriker, Padfoot or Shug Monkey. The famous "Hound of the Baskervilles" certainly shares some of the Bargheust's pedigree.

The Original Ghost Walk of Whitby.

Should you be unfortunate enough, during your travels in North Yorkshire, to stumble upon a Bargheust or even hear one howl, then you or a member of your immediate family is most certainly doomed! Local folklore has it that when the fisherman went down to the docks, during stormy weather, they would see the Bargheust trotting backwards and forwards in front of the boats. This was a clear warning that if they went to sea that particular day they would never return. The fishermens wives at home going about their daily business would often hear the Bargheust howl and know for sure that they would never ever see their husbands again. I am moderately certain that more than a few of these fishwives would have breathed rather large sighs of relief.

A certain level of superstition among fishing communities was inevitable considering the daily dangers these individuals faced and the unpredictability of their working environment. To list these superstitions would fill a book in itself - if not several books! Turning back home if one saw a woman or a female relative on the way to a boat, countless taboo words, and a belief in strange creatures such as mermaids were all part of the way of life of the old-fashioned seafarers.

A few of these superstitions and prohibitions are listed below:

The fisherman's wife would not do her washing on a sailing day for fear of "washing her man away";
Ships should not sail on Fridays;

The loss of a hat overboard signified a long trip, whilst taking a timepiece to sea signified bad luck;

Fishermen refused to sail if they saw a rat come ashore off their vessel - assuming that the rat knew something they didn't!

Never stirring tea with a knife or fork;

Never crossing knives on the galley table and avoiding laying a broom on top of the nets.

Priests or Vicars (known to fishermen as "sky-pilots") were unwelcome on board vessels.

Old lobster pots at Spital Bridge.

Although there are many tales of mermen and mermaids in fishing communities, stories containing any kind of hard evidence are a little thin on the ground. I have heard tales from locals about how their grandfathers had held conversations with mermen whilst mending nets at Saltwick Nab. However, I have only found one documented tale from this area about such creatures.

The West Cliff lighthouse.

In 1535, at nearby Skinningrove, a merman was brought up in one of the local fisherman's nets. He was taken back to the village where he was treated with great kindness. There is no description of his physical attributes except he could not speak and would only eat fish. Records have it the merman had an eye for the ladies. Life could not have been so good for him in Skinningrove as, one day, he sneaked off. The merman was later seen frolicking for a short while in the harbour before he dived beneath the waves and disappeared for good.

Cobbles in Whitby Harbour.

CHAPTER THREE.
The White Horse and Griffin.

The White Horse and Griffin.

We are just outside White Horse Yard of the White Horse and Griffin on Church Street. This building was originally constructed, in 1691, as a coaching house by Sir Hugh Cholmley for the Whitby to York mail run. It was the more "up market" competitor to the Black Horse further along the street. It took the name "Griffin" from the Cholmley family crest; the Cholmley's were regular White Horse patrons and made themselves very wealthy through their involvement in the local alum (a dye fixative) industry.

During its heyday, this place was Whitby's equivalent to the Hilton Hotel and anyone who was anyone, who came to stay in Whitby, stayed in this building. Charles Dickens resided here as did Bram Stoker, the author of "Dracula". Alfred Lord Tennyson lodged in its best rooms and Lewis Carroll was one of its patrons. At the time Carroll was staying here his suite overlooked the yard which was liberally covered with old oyster shells. This author was so captivated by the sight of all these oyster shells that he was inspired to write his famous poem the "Walrus and the Carpenter".

There is a mail room in the White Horse and Griffin, a bleak square room with a steel gate, which was often used to house local criminals; the less fortunate offenders were sent to the gallows in York, others were deported to Australia.

During the 18th century, the White Horse and Griffin was an important meeting place for members of the local smuggling fraternity. Sadly, it was the inn's success as a drinking establishment that led to its downfall. In 1945, it was closed down due to after hours drinking and the rowdy behaviour of its patrons. The White Horse and Griffin reopened in the 1987, for one season, as a waxworks' museum. It has now been converted back to its original condition as an Inn.

This hostelry happens to possess at least three ghosts. The first of these I would like to mention is the ghost of the old Landlady, a Mrs Bowler, who was around in the late nineteenth century. In life, she was a rather fearsome woman and very much prone to taking an instant liking for, or disliking to, people on first sighting. Also, it was said that she would never ever change her mind no matter how many times she met them. One particular cold frosty morning, Mrs Bowler was walking down the steps at the side of the building when she slipped, cracked her head and died, I guess rather horribly, as a result of the fall.

The ghost of the old landlady is very rarely seen, however, she does make her presence felt in another way. Should you go into the White Horse and Griffin for the first time ever you will immediately feel either very welcome or very unwelcome - never anything in between! Such is the strength of her presence it is certain that this will never change no matter how many times you visit the building.

The cellar at the front of the building is most certainly haunted by the ghost of a serving maid, known to the regulars by the name of Sarah. In life, she was a very clumsy girl and it was her clumsiness that sealed her fate. She was walking through the entrance of the building when she tripped and fell through the beer hatch straight onto the cellar floor where she broke her neck and died instantly.

One rather gruesome version of this tale suggests that Sarah was with child by the Landlord's son, and he, being a carefree fun-loving chap, resented the possibility of any future ties. It was said this son had a callous streak and it has been suggested that, rather than marry Sarah, he pushed her through the beer hatch and into the darkness of the cold dark cellar where certain oblivion awaited her on the hard stone floor. She was later found in a crumpled heap and her neck was clearly broken. To this very day, Sarah the serving maid haunts the cellar of the White Horse and Griffin.

Sarah is not seen very often, however, she does have a rather sweet habit of grabbing unsuspecting visitors to the cellar by the shoulders and giving them a jolly good squeeze.

The top floor of this building is haunted by the ghost of an old sea captain, and he is seen quite frequently. His uniform dates him within the 18th century according to descriptions given by those who have witnessed his manifestations. Shortly before he appears, the top floor of the building develops an iciness that cuts through to the bone.

The old sea captain has one outstanding feature - a great love of keys. Any guests staying on the top floor of this building are well advised not to leave keys lying around because the old sea captain will most certainly have them, and they will never be seen again. This is a fact that many guests at the White Horse and Griffin will verify after having found themselves locked inside their rooms with no means of exit.

The ghostly influence of the White Horse and Griffin extends well beyond its walls. At the neighbouring cottages, near the old White Horse Yard stables, the ghostly whinnying of the horses that used to pull the mail carriages can still be heard on many a chilly night.

The Grand Turk figurehead.

CHAPTER FOUR.
The 199 Steps and Dracula.

We are at the base of the 199 steps, and it is beyond any shadow of a doubt that there are 199 of them. Interestingly, there were only 191 when the famous preacher John Wesley visited Whitby. The present 199 steps are very much in the same condition as they were when the famous Victorian photographer Frank Meadows Sutcliffe was alive.

Curiously, countless generations of locals and visitors have walked up these steps with a view to counting them. Should you decide to walk up the steps yourselves with a view to counting them, and having reached the top, have a figure perhaps of 198 or maybe even 200, then you have two possible choices open to you. The first is to accept a rather short but unavoidable spell of bad luck, the second choice is to walk all the way back down again and then walk back up counting them correctly. There is, of course, a third choice which is the one I prefer to take - just do not bother counting in the first place.

If you think walking up the steps is hard work bear in mind that most Whitby peoples last journey was up these steps in a wooden box to St Mary's Churchyard. This was known as being "sided out" because they had to carry coffins sideways up the steep steps. You will notice, as you climb up the 199 steps, that rests have been put there for coffin bearers and that these rests get closer together the nearer you get to the top. It was traditional for Whitby brides who were being married in St Mary's Church to go up the 199 steps in full wedding dress to their wedding ceremony, the invention of the automobile has long since put paid to this tradition. In 1892, George Broderick, a truly remarkable local gentleman actually managed to hop up all of the 199 steps on one leg without stopping. God knows why!

Standing here near the top of the 199 steps we have commanding views of Whitby, and it was these vast panoramas that greatly inspired the famous novelist Bram Stoker. It is worth remembering that the Whitby of Stoker's time was somewhat different to the town we see today. Back then, a dark pall of coal smoke hung over the town and the harbour was full of rigged ships. There were considerably more cottages in Whitby than there are today, many of these were demolished in the 1960s as unfit for human habitation.

Sadly, much evidence of the Victorian town's seedy underbelly has been lost; it was reckoned the town may have had as many as seven brothels in the late nineteenth century. Inns such as The Steam Packet and The Venus are now long gone although some old inns such as The Ship, The Pier Inn and The Star are still extant.

The Grand Turk in Whitby Harbour.

Bram Stoker wrote his novel Dracula between the years of 1890 and 1896. Since the novel's publication it has never ever been out of print, not only that it has given birth to a whole industry arriving at such unusual things as the vegetarian Count Duckula and Buffy the Vampire Slayer.

Although, strictly speaking, Dracula is a fictional story some parts of this story are based in fact. Dracula arrives in Whitby in the wreckage of the Demeter, during a storm, and this fictional ship crashes into the end of Tate Hill Pier. This event was based on an actual happening when in 1868, during a ferocious storm, a Russian Schooner, The Dmitri of Narva, was blown into Whitby harbour and grounded itself on Tate Hill Beach on the east side of the town. That Stoker's Dracula arrived in Whitby disguised in the form of a large black dog was no accident - this was based on the legend of the Bargheust hound. Bram Stoker was a keen enthusiast for Whitby ghost stories and legends and most of what you have heard on the Ghost Walk tonight, Bram Stoker would have heard himself.

A view of Whitby Abbey from St Mary's Churchyard.

A lot of people credit Bram Stoker with the invention of the character of Dracula, nothing could be further from the truth. Bram Stoker was a keen student of Romanian history and, during the course of his studies, he came across an almost forgotten fifteenth century Romanian prince known as Vlad the Impaler (1431-1476). Both Vlad the Impaler and his father were both successful crusaders against the Muslim Turks. The Holy Roman Emperor was so impressed by their efforts that he awarded Vlad's father a title for his services to Christianity - "Dracul". This basically meant he was a member of "The Order of the Dragon". To be a Dracul was a distinction awarded only to the most pious and committed crusaders.

When Vlad's father was assassinated, and his eldest brother blinded with red-hot pokers and buried alive, the title was passed on to the young Vlad himself. It was traditional in Romania, at that time, for a young man inheriting his father's title to add an A to it, hence the title Dracul became Dracula.

Vlad Dracula makes Stokers fictional character seem somewhat tame. He would impale many thousands of his Turkish enemies whilst holding open air feasts for his friends and relations. He was rather fussy about how his victims impaled bodies were presented, he liked them displayed high up on hillsides and arranged in pretty patterns such as interlacing crosses, circles and squares. Dining and impaling seemed to be linked activities in the mind of Vlad.

As you can imagine all these impaled bodies smelt rather noxious! Woe betide anyone who dared to complain about the smell of rotting flesh, Vlad would have them taken to one side by his soldiers who would then impale them on a very long pole to place them above the putrid stench.

Other hobbies and interests included boiling up large cauldrons of human heads and, technically, Vlad Dracula was a vampire, on several occasions he was seen to dip his bread in the blood of his victims. It was considered a very poor career move to take Vlad Dracula bad news - under such circumstances you would leave his company with your hat nailed rather firmly to your head.

St Mary's Churchyard.

If you could imagine a terrible deed Vlad Dracula did it, and as you can also imagine he came to a rather bad end. In 1476, he was ambushed by his Turkish enemies and beheaded, his head being dispatched to the Turkish capital, Constantinople, where it was displayed on a spear to show the Turkish people that the dreaded impaler was dead. His headless corpse was buried within the walls of a monastery at Snagov in Romania. So now, sadly, everyone knows he is not buried in St Mary's Churchyard despite the popular myth (bandied around in the tourist season) that purports he is.

When Bram Stoker wrote Dracula, he certainly did his research. He based the female vampires in his story, and to some extent the Count himself, on a seventeenth century Hungarian Countess known as Elizabeth of Bathory (1560-1614).

Not only was Elizabeth fabulously wealthy and powerful, she was also very beautiful. It is believed she became brutalized at the age of six when she saw a gypsy stitched alive into the belly of a dead horse as punishment for selling his children to the Turks. Elizabeth was married to the famous crusader Count Ferenc Nasasdy who was a violent and unrefined character. It is believed that Nasasdy introduced her to the art of torture, a pursuit she was to embrace wholeheartedly!

Elizabeth's life was to take a radical turn when, as legend has it, she was out horse riding in the lands surrounding her castle at Csejte. It was during this excursion that she came upon an old witch who was blocking her path. Elizabeth, as well as being beautiful, was cursed with an inability to control her moods and prone to bouts of great irritation. Burdened by such emotions, she felt compelled to take her horse whip to the aged and wizened sorceress. The witch, rendered bloody and beaten, understandably cursed Elizabeth to her face implying that one day she would become as old and ugly as the witch herself. Elizabeth rode away from the witch a very troubled woman.

This curse must have gone rather deep because Elizabeth found herself in front of the mirror for many hours checking for lines and wrinkles until it seemed, as if by pure accident, she had discovered the secret of eternal youth. She had been beating one of her serving maids, which was a regular occurrence, and she had beaten this poor girl so badly that she had actually bled onto Elizabeth's hands. After Elizabeth had washed the blood away, she observed that her skin looked rather younger and much fresher as a result of this violent incident.

View from near St Mary's Churchyard. Arch and fence built by Pete Budd.

This event so inspired Elizabeth that she felt compelled, with the aid of accomplices and a local sorceress called Dorca, to kidnap Hungarian peasant girls which she tortured and callously drained of their blood. This she bathed in, presumably as a regular beauty treatment, and for a number of years this activity did appear to abate any signs of aging.

Briefly, she was able to forget the witch's curse!

However, as time marched on, she began to notice the odd line and the odd wrinkle upon her lovely face. Inevitably, she was forced to ask her accomplices what the problem might be, and they suggested that maybe the blood of peasant girls was not quite good enough for her purposes. These heartless associates suggested that she needed to bathe in rather better blood, and they proposed to her that she opened, at Csejte castle, a finishing school for aristocrats daughters. It goes without saying that these girls were most certainly finished when they got there.

Kidnapping peasant girls was one thing in seventeenth century Hungary, doing likewise with aristocrats daughters that was quite another. It was not long before Elizabeth was brought to trial, but not before she had worked her way through 653 girls. She had actually kept a hand written record of all her victims and the details of their gruesome deaths. As Elizabeth's blood-lust had grown, so had her casual attitude to disposing of the bodies of those she mutilated. At the time of her arrest, the remains of young girls were found littered around the grounds of Csejte Castle.

However, Elizabeth was not to be executed for her crimes! She was an aristocrat and the

Hungarian constitution of the time protected those of noble birth from execution.

Tombstones in St Mary's Churchyard.

Instead, she was bricked up inside a room of her own castle with nothing more than a small hole in the wall through which she was fed. Elizabeth was left with little to rest her eyes upon apart from a crucifix fixed on the bare walls.

Gallows were erected at the corners of her castle to show the local peasantry that justice had been done. It is worth mentioning that when Elizabeth of Bathory died, she showed not the slightest sign of any remorse.

It is also worth mentioning that there are one or two rather practically minded local historians who will tell you that Bram Stoker dreamt up Dracula after a rather bad Whitby crab supper.

A grotesque, Cliff Street.

CHAPTER FIVE.
St Mary's Churchyard and the Bargheust Coach.

The porch of St Mary's Church.

We are stood by the relative shelter of the porch of St Mary's church which happens to possess a fine Norman doorway. If you were happening to pass this church porch, say about 200 years ago on Saint Mark's Eve - that's the 24th April just before midnight, you would have seen all the local gravediggers gathered here.

Intriguingly, the reason for the local gravediggers meeting here was that, on the very stroke of midnight itself, they expected to see a procession of ghosts walk through the church door and onto the church path. After completing this short procession, these spectres would promptly vanish into the evening mist. However, the gravediggers were not expecting to see the ghosts of people long dead - they were expecting to see the ghosts of those people who were going to die within the coming year! A practical application of what the gravediggers witnessed on Saint Mark's Eve was that they could calculate how much they were going to earn within that year, and be able to budget accordingly!

A short walk away from St Mary's Church, towards the Abbey, are two long rectangular tombstones which have carved on the ends of them the skull and crossbones, a symbol often used by pirates, commonly known as the "Jolly Roger". At this point I would like to relate to you a local folktale that might just bear directly on the bones of one of the two men buried here.

A pirate's grave in St Mary's Churchyard.

There was a Whitby man who was a pirate and it was believed that he had sailed as far as the south seas. He was a hardhearted soul and one of his more despicable deeds was to make a captain and his wife walk the plank, but not before he had instructed one of his crew to steal the captain's wife's shawl as a present for his own wife when he returned home. It is said that his return trip to Whitby was plagued by all manner of obstacles and ill omens; but return he did!

When he presented his wife with the shawl, and it was an exceedingly fine silken shawl, she was delighted. In fact, such was her delight, she said that she would only wear it for Sunday best.

Inevitably, Sunday came around and the pirate's wife put the stolen shawl on and, being a vain woman, went to the mirror to see how she looked. However, she got a very unpleasant surprise when she stared into the looking glass. Horrifyingly, the face of the captain's wife, whom her husband had forced to walk the plank, was superimposed upon her own fair reflection. Naturally, the face of the captain's wife was not that of a woman in good health; it was the visage of someone who had been left to putrefy in the sea for quite some time. This terrible vision was sufficient to derange the pirate's wife. It is said she spent the remainder of her days, alternately laughing and weeping hysterically, at the asylum near Spital Bridge.

Although St Mary's churchyard is the burial ground of a fishing community, it was a rare occurrence for a sailor to be buried here. I shall explain why. In 1820, the Scarborough Evening

The Original Ghost Walk of Whitby.

News reported that out of every 16 sailors alive in the Whitby area 11 of them would either be maimed, or die, in accidents related to the fishing trade. As a result of this, it was not unusual for local fishing families to conduct a funeral without a body to bury.

The bonafide burial of sailor in St Mary's churchyard would occasion the appearance of a fantastic spectre known as the Bargheust Coach. Bargheust is a very old local word for a ghost or spook of any kind and was pronounced, in the nineteenth century, by Whitby natives, as "Boh ghost".

Sailors tombstones in St Mary's church yard.

This spectral carriage would appear on Green Lane, just behind the Abbey, and was said to be an ornate black coach drawn by six black horses. Its drivers were two wraith-like coachmen who carried flaming torches. Some versions of this tale speak of demonic outriders flanking the coach and the coachmen being headless!

The Bargheust Coach would then proceed into St Mary's churchyard where it would stop with a shuddering halt at the side of the sailor's fresh grave. From this monstrous vehicle would then climb down ghostly mourners dressed in black. These would then solemnly circle the sailors grave three times in an anti-clockwise direction. On the third circuit of the grave, the spirit, or ghost, of the dead sailor would rise up from his coffin below the soil. He would then proceed to greet the mourners on the surface before climbing into the coach with them. Interestingly, one variant on this tale states that the mourners actually dug up the body of the sailor with their bare hands.

The Bargheust Coach then weaved through the churchyard, to the very top of the 199 steps, before hurtling down them at great speed. Having reached the bottom of the steps, the coach made what could only be described as a rather nifty right turn onto Henrietta Street. It then careered along the whole length of this narrow street with considerable haste. Finally, the coach headed directly for the edge of the cliff and plunged into the foaming sea below. It is a fair assumption that the Bargheust Coach was taking the soul of the dead sailor to his proper resting place.

Prior to descending the 199 steps, I would like to take a last look at St Mary's church, it is worth remembering that there has been a place for Christian worship on this spot for over 1000 years.

The Original Ghost Walk of Whitby.

When the very first St Mary's church was built the locals of the town did a rather cruel thing, they bricked up a live animal into the foundations of this building. This animal could have been anything - a dog, a cat, a goat, a sheep or even a donkey – nobody knows for sure! However, it is known that this was a hangover from an ancient pagan pre-Christian practice of either human or animal sacrifice at the commencement of an important building project. Our superstitious ancestors believed that the spirit of this animal would act as a kind of guardian, or protector, over the whole structure of the building.

The end of Henrietta Street.

It is also said, when the very first churches in this country were being built, that the Devil would frequently interfere with the construction works. He would often demolish parts of these buildings, with kicks from his cloven hooves, during the hours of darkness.

Eventually, the local builders and masons would be forced to negotiate with the Devil. These craftsmen would usually offer the Old Nick the first living soul that entered the church, on its day of consecration, in exchange for the timely completion of the church building.

Naturally enough, the Devil was very pleased with this deal as the first living soul to enter the church on the day of consecration would be the minister. As is often the case in these tales, the builders were rather more cunning than the Devil and an animal was coaxed to lead the procession into the church on the day of consecration. As the deal stood, the Devil had no choice other than to make do with its soul rather than that of the minister.

Unusual cast iron tomb in St Mary's Churchyard.

The Original Ghost Walk of Whitby.

In time, the spirit of this unfortunate creature, for reasons never made clear by storytellers or folklorists, became known as a local ghost which was called the Church Grim. The Grim was a spectre which could only by seen by the minister of St Mary's church and only under certain circumstances.

When a funeral had occurred in the churchyard and all the mourners had departed from the graveside, the minister would glance towards the top of the church tower. There he would see the Grim, in the form of an animal, which would either be looking upwards or downwards - depending on the destination of the soul of the recently deceased person.

Whitby Abbey Interior. The ghost of Hilda is seen in the top right window space.

CHAPTER SIX.
St Hilda, the Serpents and Whitby Abbey Bells.

Whitby Abbey.

For those of us here who would find an encounter with a spectre during nighttime hours a daunting prospect, there is afforded at Whitby Abbey the opportunity to see a ghost by broad daylight. If you enter the Abbey building between the hours of 11.00am and 2.00pm and then stand facing towards the altar, whilst looking up to the top right window space, you will see the ghost of Saint Hilda. Within that space you should be able to view a woman in nun's habit with her face, hands and the folds of cloth quite clearly visible.

The Original Ghost Walk of Whitby.

It's worth mentioning that in 1936 a local gent, one Mr Hutchinson, saw the ghost of Hilda and captured her on photographic plate.

Hilda of Whitby (614 – 680) is a Christian saint and was the founding abbess of the first monastery at Whitby. In 664, the Synod of Whitby was held at the monastery and this led to the creation of the present Christian calendar. Hilda was a vital figure in the conversion of England to Christianity, she also established Whitby as one of the most important centres of learning within the Christian world. It was at Hilda's monastery that Caedmon, the first major English poet, had his mystical vision that led to his gift with words.

Statue of Caedmon by Darren Yeadon.

Icthyosaur carved by Darren Yeadon on the West Pier.

Legend has it that when Hilda arrived in Whitby she had expected work on the monastery to be well under way. This was not the case! The local stonemasons were afraid to begin building as the plain at the top of the East Cliffs was infested by a plague of venomous serpents. Such creatures held no fear for Hilda who requested only a whip to deal with them. It is said that with this whip she forcibly drove the serpents towards the edge of the cliff with the hope of driving them into the sea.

Eventually, the serpents were forced right up to the cliff edge, however, they reared up and faced Hilda defiantly. Hilda, equally defiant, lashed out at them with her whip and neatly cut their heads off with one deft stroke. The serpents, writhing in agony, then fell over the edge of the cliff onto First Bight where their petrified remains can be found to this day.

It does not take a professional folklorist to work out that this legend refers to Hilda driving serpent worshipers out of Whitby. Serpent worshiping cults were very prevalent in pagan England and Ireland, think of Saint Patrick and how he drove the snakes out of the Emerald Isle.

The petrified serpents we can still find on the beaches, and embedded in the cliffs, around Whitby are, in fact, the remains of fossil molluscs called ammonites. Fittingly, these very closely resemble headless snakes. Ammonites are also known as "Druids Eggs" and are believed to cure headaches. There are many other types of Jurassic fossils (approximately 250 million years old) to be found in the area including squid, seashells, plant fossils and marine reptiles.

The East Cliff where fossils can be found.

In pre-Darwinian times, these ancient relics were often referred to as "Sports of the Devil" being thought to be the remains of creatures that the Devil had failed to bring to life.

One common fossil found in the Whitby area is Jet. Pitch black and shiny, jet is the petrified remains of an ancient type of Monkey Puzzle tree; it is light, easily carved and takes a fine polish. Whitby is famous for its jet jewellers and there are many jet carvers presently working in the town. Incidentally, the smoke from burning jet is believed to have the power to drive away evil spirits. Interestingly, carrying jet protects the bearer against snake bites.

When King Henry the Eighth decided to close down, or dissolve, all the abbeys and monasteries he had a very keen eye on Whitby Abbey. This was not just because of the Abbey treasures and lands, but because of the Abbey bells. Whitby Abbey was one of the very first religious houses in the country to get a set of bells, and they were believed to be incredibly sweet sounding. At that time, a sweet sounding bell was supposed to have the power to drive away evil. Naturally, the people of Whitby had a great sentimental attachment for the bells.

Not a soul in Whitby knew that King Henry had sent a ship from London to come and collect the bells. However, I suspect Henry's ally Thomas Challoner (who stole the recipe for making alum from the Pope's alum workers) knew of the ship's impending arrival.

It was said that it was a shock for the locals when the ship arrived in the harbour. However, it

The Original Ghost Walk of Whitby.

was even more of a shock when the children of Whitby were seen, perhaps in a moment of unconscious clairvoyance, singing and dancing, down on the docks, that the Abbey bells were drowning and that the bells would surely drown.

Inevitably, Henry's ship arrived and the Abbey bells were loaded on board of the vessel. It set sail, on a lovely calm day, southward along the coast in the direction of Saltwick Nab. The ship did not get very far - it mysteriously sank like a stone, and to this very day, the ship and the Abbey bells remain at the bottom of the sea.

Some people believe a small fortune lies beneath the waves between Whitby and Saltwick Nab. It is supposed that not only were the Abbey bells on board of the ship but also treasures from Rievaulx and Fountains abbeys.

As a result of this event in history, there is a rather charming piece of local folklore. Should you go down to Saltwick Nab, on Saint Valentine's Day, and close your eyes whilst dreaming of the person you would most like to marry, then you might hear the Abbey bells ringing away gently below the waves. This is a sure sign that you will most certainly get together with that person.

I do think its only fair I add, there are one or two cynical local people who will tell you that what you are most likely to hear is the bell on the mile buoy marker.

Before we leave St Mary's Church, please take the trouble to view, at its east side, an unusual memorial to the Huntrodd family. This is a truly remarkable catalogue of coincidences and is most tender in its presentation.

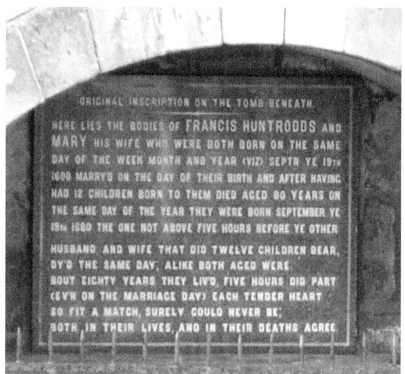

Huntrodds Memorial at St Mary's Church.

CHAPTER SEVEN.
Church Street Phantoms and the Wesley Family Ghost.

Whitby's most famous yard.

A lot of people puzzle over the name of this yard. Was it a place where families lived that could never agree? Was it a place where disputes were resolved? The truth is very simple, this is the yard of the Argument family and there are still people living in Whitby bearing this name.

Directly across Church Street, from Arguments Yard, there is a Wesleyan Chapel close by the Post Office. John Wesley (1703–1781) was reputed to have been a very popular Anglican cleric in Whitby and his meetings were extremely well attended. It was said that Wesley loved Whitby a great deal, and several Wesleyan chapels have existed in Whitby as a result of his benevolent influence. Sadly, the octagonal chapel, near the Spa Ladder area (not far from the Mussel Beds), has long since gone due to the constant erosion of the cliffs.

The Wesleyan Chapel, Church Street.

I'm sure John Wesley would have taken much humour from the following story.

It was believed that John Wesley's family had a ghost, some people also inferred that the Wesley

The Original Ghost Walk of Whitby.

family were inordinately fond of it and that it went everywhere they went. It was reckoned that the Wesley family were so fond of their ghost that they even laid it a place at the table.

When John inevitably died, the ghost was considered to be as distraught as his family members. It is said that this unhappy spirit embarked on a kind of pilgrimage to visit every place Wesley visited in his lifetime, perhaps in the hope of finding him. However, it would seem that the ghost shared John Wesley's love of Whitby, and as a result of this, the spectre, finally, came to settle here. Unsurprisingly, it chose to haunt the steps of the Wesleyan Chapel opposite Arguments yard.

Many claim that the Wesley family ghost has great powers of persuasion, and should you linger on the chapel steps being undecided as to enter or not, the ghost will, by supernatural means, persuade you to go in. I am pretty certain this whole story arose from a misunderstanding of the Wesley family habit of setting a place for "Our Good Lord" at the household table.

Whilst you are visiting Whitby it is worth viewing the yards just off Church Street, these could be the subject of a book in themselves. Try visiting New Way Ghaut, Sanders Yard, Bensons Yard, Salt Pan Well Steps (where salt was extracted from sea water) and the creepy Ellerby Lane just off Sand Gate. There are many other yards worth exploring on both sides of Whitby, every one of them has very individual characteristics.

Between White Horse Yard and the Wesleyan Chapel is Blackburn's Yard. This very attractive and broad yard holds a rather unusual and macabre surprise, a Saxon child's stone coffin used as a planter.

Saxon child's coffin.

One of the strangest stories from the Church Street area of Whitby is that of the "Phantom in Black", this happens to be a tale of a relatively recent provenance. It is known that a local man, a Mr Ingram, saw this terrifying spectre in the early hours of the morning at some point during the 1950's (I have never been able to find out the exact date).

He was employed as a "Knocker upper", a rather unfortunate term in modern parlance. His occupation was to walk along Church Street with a long pole and tap loudly on peoples bedroom windows to wake them up for their work.

Mr Ingram was turning the corner off the Market Square, just near what was then the Black

Bull Inn, onto Church Street when he felt a terrific blast of wind. The force of this was sufficient to knock him off his feet, and he fell heavily onto the cobbles.

When he picked himself up he observed, walking across the Market Square, the figure of a man, at least nine foot tall, completely dressed in black and wearing a top hat and cape. This figure strode purposefully, through the morning mist, towards the Shambles on the other side of the square. It then promptly disappeared into thin air.

Blackburn's Yard off Church Street.

This tale could be considered to be just another ghost story except it has an epilogue. On his death bed, Mr Ingram, who had been for most of his life a complete skeptic concerning the supernatural, swore on pain of going to the fiery bowels of hell that he really did see the Phantom in Black. He added that the tale he told of it did not contain a word of a lie.

The Market Square with the Black Bull Inn on the left.

Finally, Sanders Yard is believed to be haunted by the ghost of a smuggler who was murdered, literally stabbed in the back, by a close friend in a dispute over contraband. This murderous deed took place in the vaulted cellar of the yard. Pleasingly, this gloomy cavernous structure, which is most certainly several hundred years old, is still in good condition.

The smuggler's ghost is a good example of a type of spook known as a "presence", sensitive visitors to the cellar speak of experiencing an overwhelming sense of loss, or even feeling the blade of the knife that killed him against their backs.

Sanders Yard, the cellar steps are on the left.

For those of you who have an interest in smugglers, it's worth your while visiting what used to be Whitby's most famous smugglers' pub, the Old Smuggler, on Baxtergate. It is said that a secret passageway runs from the cellar of this inn to the upper harbour and that this passageway was one of the main routes for contraband to enter into the town itself. The Old Smuggler has long since ceased to be a pub and is now a café.

The Old Smuggler on Baxtergate, note the old ships carving on the right.

CHAPTER EIGHT.
Old Katy and the Hand of Glory.

Woodland at the Fitz Steps near Ruswarp.

No ghost walk tour would be complete without the mention of witches. Quaintly, there are still witches in Whitby to this day, however, most of these are of the nature loving Wiccan persuasion and not given to dark deeds or malevolence. Such is the popularity of the Wiccan faith that many of the alternative retail outlets in Whitby stock accoutrements for witches (quite possibly made in China) such as wands and magical knives.

Whitby's most memorable and feared witch was "Old Katy" (1775–1823) whose reputation extended well beyond her residence in the village of Ruswarp. She was feared by all and avoided by all, except for one individual - a pedlar called Abe Rogers.

Abe would walk many miles over the moors to vend his wares and was known by many people in the surrounding villages. He was acquainted with Katy and it is believed they had an uneasy friendship, however, one cold winter day they were to fall into complete enmity. Abe had been walking across a stretch of moorland, not far from Ruswarp, when he crossed paths with Katy, he recognized her immediately from her gait and fearsome appearance.

Sign for the Pannett Park Gallery inspired by the "Hand of Glory".

Nobody knows the cause of their disagreement, but disagree they did! So much so that Katy, deceptively strong and supple for an old hag, tried to stab Abe with a knife which she had hidden in the folds of her cape. Luckily, Abe was faster and stronger than Katy and succeeded in wrestling her to the ground.

Katy, however, was by no means beaten, as she writhed under Abe's vice-like grip she began to chant an ancient spell in a language not known to any folk other than witches. A thick fog suddenly came from nowhere and out of it marched hordes of hideous demons uttering wicked threats. Abe undaunted, leapt away from Katy and pulled from a small pouch, tied to his belt, a pinch of powder. This he threw to the ground whilst muttering a strange incantation of his own. Almost instantly a whirlwind arose which blew Katy's malevolent demons in all directions across the moors. Abe sensibly used this as an opportunity to escape.

Pannett Art Gallery and Whitby Museum.

Inside the Pannett Art Gallery and Whitby Museum is a rather gruesome relic connected with the practice of witchcraft. This is known as a Hand of Glory, and it was made from a human hand taken by a witch from an executed criminal.

The hand itself was boiled to extract its fat in order to make a candle for use at a later date. The bones and skin then had to be pickled in a mixture of zimort, saltpetre and peppercorn before finally being hung to cure in a chimney over the smoke of yew and juniper wood. I presume that if the witch had used oak chips it would have been kippered.

A Hand of Glory was a talisman of invisibility. If one placed the candle of human fat between its fingers, and lit the candle before entering the house of an adversary, they would be rendered unconscious or incapable of any movement. The Hand of Glory was considered a vital accessory for house breakers.

The Pannett Art Gallery and Whitby Museum is a truly fascinating place and well worth a visit if only to see the Hand of Glory and nothing else.

View from Pannett Park towards Bagdale.

A west side fortune telling booth.

Whitby is still in the thrall of the supernatural, as are many of its visitors, and fortune-tellers continue to ply their trade within the town as they have done for centuries. Many of these work from home and are only known of by word of mouth as it is illegal for them to advertise their services in the Whitby Gazette. This is a result of the Fraudulent Mediums Act of 1951 designed to protect vulnerable members of society from charlatans.

Others, like the very well regarded Lee Esther, dispense their prophecies on the seafront asking only for a "consideration or gift" as advertising a price for one's supernatural, or psychic services, is an invitation to fall foul of this act too!

Enjoying the sights on Whitby's west side.

CHAPTER NINE.
The Penny Hedge.

The Penny Hedge.

The legend of the Penny Hedge originates in 1159 when three hunters (Allatson, Ralph de Percy and William de Bruce) were out at Eskdaleside pursuing a wild boar. They had followed their prey for quite some distance and the boar sought refuge inside the chapel of a local hermit. The hermit, being of a kindly disposition towards animals, refused the hunters' entry. They rewarded him for his compassion by beating him with great ferocity, so much so that his wounds were most certainly mortal.

The hunters, on realizing the hermit would shortly die, begged forgiveness. They did not want the death of a holy man on their consciences and also be denied entrance into heaven when they died themselves.

Forgiveness was given to them by the godly hermit in the presence of the Abbott of Whitby. However, the hunters were pardoned only on the condition that they and their descendants performed a penance each Ascension Day Eve.

This penance involved weaving a hedge of hazel stakes which had to be planted on the east side of Whitby harbour. The hermit stipulated that the wood had to come from Eskdaleside, be cut with a knife costing one penny and that the hedge had to be strong enough to withstand three tides.

To this day the penance is still performed, and after the Penny Hedge is planted a horn blows a sonorous note followed by a shout of "Out on thee" three times.

A cold autumn day.

CHAPTER TEN.
Apocryphal and Odd Ghost Stories.

View of Whitby Abbey from Bakehouse Yard.

There is a rather well-known Whitby ghost story which does not seem to have the slightest bit of evidence to back it up. I suspect it serves as a warning about the dangers of vanity and hot ovens. This tale concerns the misfortune of "the Burning Girl".

Grape Lane with the Cook Memorial Museum.

Basically, this is a tale common to many places in England and it goes something like this. There was a young girl who worked in a bakery. She was believed to be very pretty and had the most lustrous waist length hair which she was constantly brushing and fussing over.

The terrible part of the story is that one day, whilst the girl was working near one of the ovens, she accidentally set her lovely locks on fire. Of course, she was horribly disfigured by the accident and had a slow lingering and painful demise. Years later, visitors to the bakery, usually lone females, see the girl's ghost near the ovens

The Original Ghost Walk of Whitby.

brushing her hair, and she concernedly asks them what they think of her locks before vanishing - leaving behind nothing except a burnt aroma.

Whitby has many bakeries all of which claim to be the place where this tragic tale arose. In the nineteenth century, most of the bakers ovens in Whitby were in Bakehouse Yard. Some local folklorists say the girl's accident occurred at a baker's on Grape Lane. Personally, I'd say just take your pick.

Whilst in the vicinity of Grape Lane, it is worth mentioning the Cook Memorial Museum where James Cook served his apprenticeship. Careful scrutiny of the front of the building will reveal, on the second floor, a small round window which is a fine example of rudimentary hygiene technology. It is an old toilet window from the days when toilets were cupboards with buckets in them. Presumably, the window was there so one could find and not miss the bucket. A female spectre in eighteenth century dress is frequently seen emerging from the cupboard that this window services. No sighting of her has yet been accompanied by a ghostly odour that might betray the exact nature of her activity in the cupboard.

Joking aside, there is one ghost in the Fishburn Park area of Whitby, at Cleveland Terrace, who fills the house with the smell of boiled cabbage before manifesting himself.

In my many years of researching the ghosts of Whitby, I have come across numerous reports of spectral sightings but most of these have no narrative connected with them whatsoever. For example, there is a procession of ghostly nuns that walk through Blackburn's Yard, no story to go with this though, and no clear reason for them being seen there! There's a headless monk who walks the Fitz Steps near Ruswarp, no one knows why. Many of these yarns come without dates or any kind of evident basis. Sometimes it's better to suspend all disbelief and enjoy the tale for its own sake. This brings me to the tales of the lighthouse ghosts and the White Wraith.

It is believed that both lighthouses are haunted. The West Cliff lighthouse is considered to be haunted by the ghost of a one armed fishermen who died of a heart attack on the lighthouse stairs. The story goes that in the late 1930s a young girl and her mother were walking up the lighthouse stairs, the young girl was walking in front. Suddenly, the young girl stopped dead in her tracks about half-way up. The mother inquired as to why she had stopped and the girl explained that she could see a man lying on the steps. The girl, when questioned further, described the man in detail and mentioned that he had only one arm.

Whitby Harbour.

Strangely enough, the mother knew who she was talking about, she had known of a one armed fisherman in life and also knew he had died of a heart attack on the very stairs they were climbing. Where the girl could see a prostrate body the mother could only see the lighthouse stairs, such events are not uncommon in ghost stories! What is remarkable in this tale is that the mother, who does not see the spirit, recognizes who it is.

Fishing boats in Whitby Harbour.

The tale of the East Cliff lighthouse is more romantic. It is believed that a local girl, called Sylvia Swales, used to court two brothers at this lighthouse. Both of them fell in love with her, and she with them. However, Sylvia could not for the life of her decide which one she should marry. Their father decided to settle the matter through healthy competition and suggested that they should have a boat race to settle the matter. Both brothers were in favour of this and rowed, with youthful vigour, out of the harbour mouth never to be seen alive again. Their dead bodies were washed up two days later near Saltwick Nab. To this day Sylvia is said to haunt the base of the lighthouse, and she is often seen looking longingly out to sea in the hope of catching sight of her lost loves.

I question this second story, I have some knowledge of local tides and would have thought that the brothers bodies should have been washed up somewhere further north such as Happy Valley or Sandsend.

View from West Cliff.

The mysterious White Wraith is said to appear on the West Cliff, near the Royal Hotel (made famous by the patronage of Bram Stoker and the television series "Heartbeat"). It is a luminous human shaped cloud which drifts along the edge of the cliff before falling slowly downward towards the beach where it silently disappears. Sounds a bit like fog or phosphorescence to me!

The Original Ghost Walk of Whitby.

The viaduct over the Esk.

I'd like to begin to wind up this tour with a tale that is common to the UK. Sadly, there is no real hard evidence for it.

Local legend has it that when the Viaduct was being built across the River Esk, for the Whitby to Scarborough railway line, a dreadful accident occurred. It is said that a workman slipped into one of the columns of the viaduct whilst it was being filled with cement and disappeared without trace. As it happened, the workman was single and many miles from his home and family, so the builders of the viaduct took the callous chance that he would not be missed and no effort was made to retrieve his remains.

At night, he can be heard, if you dare to press your ear against one of the viaducts columns, banging against the interior brickwork and screaming desperately to be freed.

These tales are common, for example it is said that men were accidentally riveted between steel sections into the sides of ships such as Brunel's SS Great Eastern and the Titanic, and that the cruel shipyard owners made no effort to rescue them. Such tales were used, by superstitious sailors, to explain the strange noises occurring deep within the bowels of large iron sea going steam vessels. I suspect these tales come from somewhere deep down in our collective consciousness. One only has to think of the human, or animal, sacrifice element in tales such as that of the Church Grim.

Finally, a word of warning! Should you be walking the streets of Whitby and happen to see your exact double walking towards you - beware! Chances are that you will not be seeing a long-lost twin, but something considerably more unnerving. Whitby's Waft is a spectre which appears as an exact duplicate of oneself - even down to the clothes and mannerisms. To acknowledge one's Waft is a fatal mistake as this gives it permission to steal your soul.

Obviously, the Waft is best avoided at all costs.

CHAPTER ELEVEN.
Epilogue.

The White Rabbit Steps, overlooking the Craggs.

My partner, Samantha, often says to me "You do know these ghost stories aren't real, it's all in the mind. However, people do like to believe in these things because it's fun." I always end up nodding my head in agreement because to argue the point would be far too tough.

Black Horse Yard, the Black Horse pub is on the right.

The Original Ghost Walk of Whitby.

Sometimes, when I was taking out a ghost walk tour, people asked me whether I believed in ghosts. My reply was always a glib - "Does a plumber believe in pipes?" Indeed, any amount of familiarity with one's subject can breed a certain degree of contempt. It is very easy to forget the impact that many of these tales can have on first hearing. Before you put this book down, and perhaps forget about it completely, please pay heed to the following tale.

In November 1999, I had the pleasure of taking a private party from a branch of the Spiritualist Church on the Original Ghost Walk of Whitby. The evening passed pleasantly enough. I only told a fraction of the stories I knew as my audience was far too busy picking up on the vibrations of each place at which we stopped.

There were a lot of observations made by the group, some of them seemed downright nutty to me. However, one of their comments did stick in my mind. A gentleman in his early forties remarked that our group had been followed, throughout the entire walk, by the spirit of an old man wearing a flat cap. He further added that there was a picture of this man in the front bar of the Black Horse pub.

I had heard stuff like this before, a lady spiritualist had said to me, some years previously, that I was being followed by the spirit of a woman dressed in black who I had met on holiday a while back. Furthermore, this woman happened to have recently passed way and that there was some connection with eggs! Strangely enough, I had met a very old lady dressed in black whilst on holiday in Crete and "yes" she had given me some eggs from the chickens she kept as pets. I was impressed!

Two months later, in 2000, something very strange happened. I was completing the Ghost Walk in Sanders Yard and received a very feisty round of applause the very moment I wound up the tour. The response of my audience to my efforts was far above and beyond what I might have expected. Shortly afterwards, a well presented gentleman asked me "How did you do that?"

I was confused, and inquired as to what I had done. He said, with a most factual tone, that an old man, wearing a flat cap, had walked out of the shadows and stood behind me as though he was listening to the tour. He added that just before I had finished the tour this old man had, to use his words, "vanished into thin air". The gentleman continued to add that he had been on many ghost tours and that this was the best special effect he had ever seen.

Finally, he mentioned that the old man bore a striking resemblance to a picture he had seen in the front bar of the Black Horse just before the tour, and demanded to know if I had arranged this on purpose. Understandably, I didn't know what to say as my tour guest spoke with utter sincerity. I wasn't afforded the chance to question other members of the audience as to what they may or may not have seen, they had long since evaporated into the thick darkness of the night.

The gentleman smiled and bid me farewell. I stood there and mused over the intriguing possibility that a ghost had appeared on the tour and that I, the guide, had not seen it.

I rest my case.

"From Ghosties and Ghoulies may the Good Lord Deliver Us".

An old English prayer.

Many thanks to Mark Graham (The Original Ghost Walk of York), Michael Wray (The Original Ghost Walk of Whitby), Samantha, the Ritson family, Peter Wilson, John Corby, Maureen Clark, Harry Collett (for reminding me what not to do!), Geordie Paul, Mick and Angie of the Whitby Folk Club, Vasey, Fossil Shop Dave, Joy Peach and countless others for their unconditional support and encouragement.

THE END.

Cineri gloria sera venit.

Printed in Great Britain
by Amazon